The Complete Book of Republican Wisdom and Knowledge

By Peter Klein

Warning!

This is not a serious exposition but is only meant for amusement.

For further information contact Ravenwolf Publishing c/o Peter Klein
PO Book 116,
Indian Lake, NY, 12842
ravenwolfpublishing@gmail.com

Indiana State Treasurer Richard Mourdock said, "Even when life begins in that horrible situation of rape, that is something that God intended to happen"

The above was just to start the conversation. The following pages are blank for you to list more words of Republican wisdom or you can use the pages to draw and color or use as a date book or journal.

The following pages are blank for you to list more words of Republican wisdom or you can use the pages to draw and color of use as a date book or journal.

The following pages are blank for you to list more words of Republican wisdom or you can use the pages to draw and color of use as a date book or journal.

The following pages are blank for you to list more words of Republican wisdom or you can use the pages to draw and color of use as a date book or journal.

The following pages are blank for you to list more words of Republican wisdom or you can use the pages to draw and color of use as a date book or journal.

The following pages are blank for you to list more words of Republican wisdom or you can use the pages to draw and color of use as a date book or journal.

The following pages are blank for you to list more words of Republican wisdom or you can use the pages to draw and color of use as a date book or journal.

The following pages are blank for you to list more words of Republican wisdom or you can use the pages to draw and color of use as a date book or journal.

The following pages are blank for you to list more words of Republican wisdom or you can use the pages to draw and color of use as a date book or journal.

The following pages are blank for you to list more words of Republican wisdom or you can use the pages to draw and color of use as a date book or journal.

The following pages are blank for you to list more words of Republican wisdom or you can use the pages to draw and color of use as a date book or journal.

The following pages are blank for you to list more words of Republican wisdom or you can use the pages to draw and color of use as a date book or journal.

The following pages are blank for you to list more words of Republican wisdom or you can use the pages to draw and color of use as a date book or journal.

The following pages are blank for you to list more words of Republican wisdom or you can use the pages to draw and color of use as a date book or journal.

The following pages are blank for you to list more words of Republican wisdom or you can use the pages to draw and color of use as a date book or journal.

The following pages are blank for you to list more words of Republican wisdom or you can use the pages to draw and color of use as a date book or journal.

The following pages are blank for you to list more words of Republican wisdom or you can use the pages to draw and color of use as a date book or journal.

The following pages are blank for you to list more words of Republican wisdom or you can use the pages to draw and color of use as a date book or journal.

The following pages are blank for you to list more words of Republican wisdom or you can use the pages to draw and color of use as a date book or journal.

The following pages are blank for you to list more words of Republican wisdom or you can use the pages to draw and color of use as a date book or journal.

The following pages are blank for you to list more words of Republican wisdom or you can use the pages to draw and color of use as a date book or journal.

The following pages are blank for you to list more words of Republican wisdom or you can use the pages to draw and color of use as a date book or journal.

The following pages are blank for you to list more words of Republican wisdom or you can use the pages to draw and color of use as a date book or journal.

The following pages are blank for you to list more words of Republican wisdom or you can use the pages to draw and color of use as a date book or journal.

The following pages are blank for you to list more words of Republican wisdom or you can use the pages to draw and color of use as a date book or journal.

The following pages are blank for you to list more words of Republican wisdom or you can use the pages to draw and color of use as a date book or journal.

The following pages are blank for you to list more words of Republican wisdom or you can use the pages to draw and color of use as a date book or journal.

The following pages are blank for you to list more words of Republican wisdom or you can use the pages to draw and color of use as a date book or journal.

The following pages are blank for you to list more words of Republican wisdom or you can use the pages to draw and color of use as a date book or journal.

The following pages are blank for you to list more words of Republican wisdom or you can use the pages to draw and color of use as a date book or journal.

The following pages are blank for you to list more words of Republican wisdom or you can use the pages to draw and color of use as a date book or journal.

The following pages are blank for you to list more words of Republican wisdom or you can use the pages to draw and color of use as a date book or journal.

The following pages are blank for you to list more words of Republican wisdom or you can use the pages to draw and color of use as a date book or journal.

The following pages are blank for you to list more words of Republican wisdom or you can use the pages to draw and color of use as a date book or journal.

The following pages are blank for you to list more words of Republican wisdom or you can use the pages to draw and color of use as a date book or journal.

The following pages are blank for you to list more words of Republican wisdom or you can use the pages to draw and color of use as a date book or journal.

The following pages are blank for you to list more words of Republican wisdom or you can use the pages to draw and color of use as a date book or journal.

The following pages are blank for you to list more words of Republican wisdom or you can use the pages to draw and color of use as a date book or journal.

The following pages are blank for you to list more words of Republican wisdom or you can use the pages to draw and color of use as a date book or journal.

The following pages are blank for you to list more words of Republican wisdom or you can use the pages to draw and color of use as a date book or journal.

The following pages are blank for you to list more words of Republican wisdom or you can use the pages to draw and color of use as a date book or journal.

The following pages are blank for you to list more words of Republican wisdom or you can use the pages to draw and color of use as a date book or journal.

The following pages are blank for you to list more words of Republican wisdom or you can use the pages to draw and color of use as a date book or journal.

The following pages are blank for you to list more words of Republican wisdom or you can use the pages to draw and color of use as a date book or journal.

The following pages are blank for you to list more words of Republican wisdom or you can use the pages to draw and color of use as a date book or journal.

The following pages are blank for you to list more words of Republican wisdom or you can use the pages to draw and color of use as a date book or journal.

The following pages are blank for you to list more words of Republican wisdom or you can use the pages to draw and color of use as a date book or journal.

The following pages are blank for you to list more words of Republican wisdom or you can use the pages to draw and color of use as a date book or journal.

The following pages are blank for you to list more words of Republican wisdom or you can use the pages to draw and color of use as a date book or journal.

The following pages are blank for you to list more words of Republican wisdom or you can use the pages to draw and color of use as a date book or journal.

The following pages are blank for you to list more words of Republican wisdom or you can use the pages to draw and color of use as a date book or journal.

The following pages are blank for you to list more words of Republican wisdom or you can use the pages to draw and color of use as a date book or journal.

The following pages are blank for you to list more words of Republican wisdom or you can use the pages to draw and color of use as a date book or journal.

The following pages are blank for you to list more words of Republican wisdom or you can use the pages to draw and color of use as a date book or journal.

The following pages are blank for you to list more words of Republican wisdom or you can use the pages to draw and color of use as a date book or journal.

The following pages are blank for you to list more words of Republican wisdom or you can use the pages to draw and color of use as a date book or journal.

The following pages are blank for you to list more words of Republican wisdom or you can use the pages to draw and color of use as a date book or journal.

The following pages are blank for you to list more words of Republican wisdom or you can use the pages to draw and color of use as a date book or journal.

The following pages are blank for you to list more words of Republican wisdom or you can use the pages to draw and color of use as a date book or journal.

The following pages are blank for you to list more words of Republican wisdom or you can use the pages to draw and color of use as a date book or journal.

The following pages are blank for you to list more words of Republican wisdom or you can use the pages to draw and color of use as a date book or journal.

The following pages are blank for you to list more words of Republican wisdom or you can use the pages to draw and color of use as a date book or journal.

The following pages are blank for you to list more words of Republican wisdom or you can use the pages to draw and color of use as a date book or journal.

The following pages are blank for you to list more words of Republican wisdom or you can use the pages to draw and color of use as a date book or journal.

The following pages are blank for you to list more words of Republican wisdom or you can use the pages to draw and color of use as a date book or journal.

The following pages are blank for you to list more words of Republican wisdom or you can use the pages to draw and color of use as a date book or journal.

The following pages are blank for you to list more words of Republican wisdom or you can use the pages to draw and color of use as a date book or journal.

The following pages are blank for you to list more words of Republican wisdom or you can use the pages to draw and color of use as a date book or journal.

The following pages are blank for you to list more words of Republican wisdom or you can use the pages to draw and color of use as a date book or journal.

The following pages are blank for you to list more words of Republican wisdom or you can use the pages to draw and color of use as a date book or journal.

The following pages are blank for you to list more words of Republican wisdom or you can use the pages to draw and color of use as a date book or journal.

The following pages are blank for you to list more words of Republican wisdom or you can use the pages to draw and color of use as a date book or journal.

The following pages are blank for you to list more words of Republican wisdom or you can use the pages to draw and color of use as a date book or journal.

The following pages are blank for you to list more words of Republican wisdom or you can use the pages to draw and color of use as a date book or journal.

The following pages are blank for you to list more words of Republican wisdom or you can use the pages to draw and color of use as a date book or journal.

The following pages are blank for you to list more words of Republican wisdom or you can use the pages to draw and color of use as a date book or journal.

The following pages are blank for you to list more words of Republican wisdom or you can use the pages to draw and color of use as a date book or journal.

The following pages are blank for you to list more words of Republican wisdom or you can use the pages to draw and color of use as a date book or journal.

The following pages are blank for you to list more words of Republican wisdom or you can use the pages to draw and color of use as a date book or journal.

The following pages are blank for you to list more words of Republican wisdom or you can use the pages to draw and color of use as a date book or journal.

The following pages are blank for you to list more words of Republican wisdom or you can use the pages to draw and color of use as a date book or journal.

The following pages are blank for you to list more words of Republican wisdom or you can use the pages to draw and color of use as a date book or journal.

The following pages are blank for you to list more words of Republican wisdom or you can use the pages to draw and color of use as a date book or journal.

The following pages are blank for you to list more words of Republican wisdom or you can use the pages to draw and color of use as a date book or journal.

The following pages are blank for you to list more words of Republican wisdom or you can use the pages to draw and color of use as a date book or journal.

The following pages are blank for you to list more words of Republican wisdom or you can use the pages to draw and color of use as a date book or journal.

The following pages are blank for you to list more words of Republican wisdom or you can use the pages to draw and color of use as a date book or journal.

The following pages are blank for you to list more words of Republican wisdom or you can use the pages to draw and color of use as a date book or journal.

The following pages are blank for you to list more words of Republican wisdom or you can use the pages to draw and color of use as a date book or journal.

The following pages are blank for you to list more words of Republican wisdom or you can use the pages to draw and color of use as a date book or journal.

The following pages are blank for you to list more words of Republican wisdom or you can use the pages to draw and color of use as a date book or journal.

The following pages are blank for you to list more words of Republican wisdom or you can use the pages to draw and color of use as a date book or journal.

The following pages are blank for you to list more words of Republican wisdom or you can use the pages to draw and color of use as a date book or journal.

The following pages are blank for you to list more words of Republican wisdom or you can use the pages to draw and color of use as a date book or journal.

The following pages are blank for you to list more words of Republican wisdom or you can use the pages to draw and color of use as a date book or journal.

The following pages are blank for you to list more words of Republican wisdom or you can use the pages to draw and color of use as a date book or journal.

The following pages are blank for you to list more words of Republican wisdom or you can use the pages to draw and color of use as a date book or journal.

The following pages are blank for you to list more words of Republican wisdom or you can use the pages to draw and color of use as a date book or journal.

The following pages are blank for you to list more words of Republican wisdom or you can use the pages to draw and color of use as a date book or journal.

The following pages are blank for you to list more words of Republican wisdom or you can use the pages to draw and color of use as a date book or journal.

The following pages are blank for you to list more words of Republican wisdom or you can use the pages to draw and color of use as a date book or journal.

The following pages are blank for you to list more words of Republican wisdom or you can use the pages to draw and color of use as a date book or journal.

The following pages are blank for you to list more words of Republican wisdom or you can use the pages to draw and color of use as a date book or journal.

The following pages are blank for you to list more words of Republican wisdom or you can use the pages to draw and color of use as a date book or journal.

The following pages are blank for you to list more words of Republican wisdom or you can use the pages to draw and color of use as a date book or journal.

The following pages are blank for you to list more words of Republican wisdom or you can use the pages to draw and color of use as a date book or journal.

The following pages are blank for you to list more words of Republican wisdom or you can use the pages to draw and color of use as a date book or journal.

The following pages are blank for you to list more words of Republican wisdom or you can use the pages to draw and color of use as a date book or journal.

The following pages are blank for you to list more words of Republican wisdom or you can use the pages to draw and color of use as a date book or journal.

The following pages are blank for you to list more words of Republican wisdom or you can use the pages to draw and color of use as a date book or journal.

The following page is blank for you to list more words of Republican wisdom or you can use the pages to draw and color of use as a date book or journal.